Gospel Drunk

AIDAN CHAFE

Gospel
Drunk

UNIVERSITY *of* ALBERTA PRESS

Published by

University of Alberta Press
1–16 Rutherford Library South
11204 89 Avenue NW
Edmonton, Alberta, Canada T6G 2J4
uap.ualberta.ca

LIBRARY AND ARCHIVES CANADA
CATALOGUING IN PUBLICATION

Title: Gospel drunk / Aidan Chafe.
Names: Chafe, Aidan, 1983– author.
Series: Robert Kroetsch series.
Description: Series statement: Robert
    Kroetsch series | Poems.
Identifiers:
    Canadiana (print) 20200406280 |
    Canadiana (ebook) 20200406329 |
    ISBN 9781772125467 (softcover) |
    ISBN 9781772125672 (PDF)
Classification: LCC PS8605.H327 G67
2021 | DDC C811/.6—dc23

First edition, first printing, 2021.
First printed and bound in Canada by
Houghton Boston Printers, Saskatoon,
Saskatchewan.
Copyediting by Kimmy Beach.
Proofreading by Tanvi Mohile.

A volume in the Robert Kroetsch Series.

University of Alberta Press is committed
to protecting our natural environment.
As part of our efforts, this book is
printed on Enviro Paper: it contains
100% post-consumer recycled fibres and
is acid- and chlorine-free.

University of Alberta Press gratefully
acknowledges the support received
for its publishing program from
the Government of Canada, the
Canada Council for the Arts, and the
Government of Alberta through the
Alberta Media Fund.

for Reason

What is wanted are blindness and intoxication and an eternal song over the waves in which reason has drowned!

—FRIEDRICH NIETZSCHE

Contents

Disciple

As a child I fostered abandoned kites,
imagined windows opening their eyes,
the wind sneezing maple leaves into flight.
Inside my house, I washed myself under
a waterfall, rinsed my hands in a river.
I held a plastic shell to my ear to hear
the waves of your voice. My heart was late
night percussion. My mind a grab bag
of thoughts. I kept chasing the moment
like a bad detective, any bird for a dog.
Even the ocean lost me to its gurgled gossip.
At mass, when my family did their best
impression of paying attention, I turned
the TV on in my head, watched Saturday
morning cartoons. Before I said bedtime
prayers, I covered my Bible in stickers,
silenced God with radio, wondered how
many good deeds I needed for a halo.

Galileo

at recess
I discovered a lone planet
tied to a string
orbiting a metal pole

observed the heliocentric patterns
made by girl clusters

admired the brave astronauts
as I stood at a distance

universe of one

hiding a meteor of passion
inside my chest

Trust

The underbrush hissed
as my father drove his 4×4 to a clearing
several kilometres into the bush
past a legion of Douglas fir
that bowed to a lake
mythical as morning fog.

Equipped with rods, bait and tackle,
we settled on an embankment of muck,
trimming the water's tranquility
with our casts.

Nearby, a grassy islet
bridged by a floating log
called to us.

With the balance
of a lumberjack
father easily made it across,
turned, then offered me
his assured arm.

For a moment,
with the water waiting,
I believed
and in good faith
leapt.

Helmets and Gloves

In the dressing room
after practice, the team
volunteered me and another
to topple our team's Goliath.

We stood gangly, bare-chested,
taking turns swatting air
while fear swelled our thoughts.

Goliath caught the other boy
with a hurricane.
A metal cage saved his face
from the fall.

Inside our putrid temple
of ignorance and testosterone
my teammates confirmed
the righteousness of their fathers
while I looked up to see
if God was watching.

Social Development

Pressured to wear a green thong
and perform hazing rituals
in front of my peers, I learned
the price of acceptance is dignity.
That some boys get off breaking egos
glued from broken glass.
That I can house hurt in my gut.
That some substances detonate distress.
So I found father's liquor in the cabinets,
walked to high school dances half-cut.
Drowned in the pool of awkward glances.
Experimented with Bunsen burners
stolen from the science lab.
In those bushes we inhaled volumes of smoke
until our eyes turned the colour of sunset.
Giggled at the doodles we graffitied
with our piss on the neighbour's siding.
Introduced to smokeless tobacco during spare,
I spat tar sands in the parking lot.
Played puck with wads nestled in my cheek.
Discovered that skates are just boots
glued to knives. Coaches become dragons
in suits. Winning is a pill for insecurity.
Some boys are gods other boys worship.

Ode to the Hockey Bro

The hockey bro is a beachwear model
in a blizzard. Charter bus pioneer.
Small town savant. Cartographer
of provincial rinks. Napoleon of the prairies.
Prodigy of the 5 a.m. wakeup call. Wizard
of the one-night stand. Puck bunny trapper.
Farm girl Casanova. Poet of the postgame.
Fluent in fisticuff. In line brawl linguistics.
The hockey bro is a spittoon sergeant.
Red light renegade. Pavlovian for "Thunderstruck."
Sheer animal for the loose puck.

Churches, Trucks and Shallow Pools

my town boasts a liquor store
      for every church hall

preaches salvation
      in every bottle

has DUI in its DNA

waxes on about real estate,
unmoved by community

open to segregation,
closed for immigration

barely passes the Bechdel test
loves the Bible
          rarely reads it

where bravery
      is two men leaving
a house together

and the mayor manures
the homeless
        while migrants
bloody fingers picking berries

and hunter-gatherers
drive trucks on steroids
        clogging the highway's arteries
as clouds bully the sky

where twenty-somethings
high dive marriages
        into shallow pools

and parents come unassembled
with hearts
        sold separately

and children speak to gods
and ghosts

about family
missing from the portraits
of their lives

play with broken toys
dream of shinier things

Driving Through Kitsilano

I want to know how much the passing tree
is charging for its angle of shade.
A selfie beneath its twisted embrace.
Whether my last paycheque could cover
a blade of leaf, a sampling of sap.
I worry a neighbourhood toll booth
is stationed around the bend
waiting to collect luxury tax.
I remember building a tree fort
with Clayton behind his parents'
fenced-in yard out of plywood
his father took from work.
We spent a summer
swinging hammers to construct
that nine-year-old-boy conception
of architectural symmetry.
The stain of each nail's rust-red skin
disappearing until a metal circle remained.
I bled from one, the samurai of the bunch,
thrusting its sharp head out of a pile
of waterlogged wood.
Now, twenty-five years later,
I wonder if the fort's still there,
waiting for me
with my middle-class wage
to return home.

Suburban Lament

Mountains receive hair transplants:
tree follicles replaced with houses
rosaried in asphalt and giraffe-necked
lampposts. Sad clouds come down
for comfort. Tears become puddles
hiding cartoon-themed galoshes.
Children run fingers along wet railings,
bored of a traditional love for swings.
Leaves etch impressions on the
sidewalk. A dog whimpers his petition
against captivity to an authoritarian
fence. The church is fast asleep
counting sheep. The day still dark
when we awake. Our heads crest
a horizon of linen. My eyes open
to forest fires on television, yours
blink like the bedroom alarm clock
between sips of tea. Neighbours
suffocate our reputation behind
the blinds. In this severe climate
of fitness our bodies are just
a bad spell. We lie facing opposite
walls, wade into pools of data,
as rain raps its knuckles on the roof,
and the crows and raccoons
rummage undeterred for scraps.

Two Lips

In the backyard archipelago of pots
you putter away the hours,
marvelling at the flowering delights,

making stakes out of retired
badminton racquets, a severed garden hose
you arc in-and-out of soil like a snake
slithering among tiny tomato plants.

I stay indoors watering the pages.
Cultivating words. Summoned
only for celebratory occasions:
cutting of ripe tomato, opening
of premature snow pea.

On rainy days I lap up lamentations
like a dog, coddle you through casualties:
slug eyeing strawberry, mildew frothing
away pea plant. Twice a year I lend a hand

relocating ever-growing Christmas tree,
domesticate it with you for winter,
dressing it up like a traffic light
before parking it back beside its potted friends.

Only in yield, when a release of you
triggers me, do I tend to garden:
a mouth I sow kisses, seeds I see
budding in your eyes.

Fall of the Empire

When the war waged on my father's body won,
his mind retreated to the foothills of his youth.
We treated wounds, reopening as they healed.
Sutures of words passing only for bandages.
Fragility in the headwind, winding through
the corridors of his consciousness. I held
my thoughts in my hands, smoothed them
along the crimson Rorschach on his right arm.
Scoliosis, psychosis, narcolepsy—unspoken
narratives only the family knew. A story
stored in cells. In the ceaseless albatross
circling his mind, until humility, caged in the
psych ward, released his conditions for surrender.

Meditation on Enclosed Space

A room is
a refuge
     a reformatory
          a universe of thoughts
a landfill of dreams

A room
     keeps weather outside
& others away

A secret
gives birth
     in a room,
          rearing its
little rumours

A border
is a line
     on the floorboards
          in a room
with two towns

Two rooms
     are countries
divided by drywall

A room
        acts airily
               around argument,
knows
when to amplify anger

A room
gets exposed
        postmortem,
               found naked
post theft

A room
        is a timpani
of feet & water

A room is
        imagination
at night

A room is
rapture before
        a long choir
               of silence

A mother is
        the first room
we ever knew

This Might Be the Warmest Parking Lot in Canada

A mother in mittens rubs her face in a frenzy
as the habit spreads to her children in the backseat.

The car coughs, tries to get over the cold.
January with its foul mouth drives people crazy,

but I tend to look past it. Two smokers, the last of their kind,
huddle together inside an empty shopping-cart station.

One becomes a cloud while the other mutters,
Why doesn't Justin build a wall to keep out winter?

A mess of police cruisers stutter outside the coffee shop.
A lost squirrel freezes trying to find its tree.

Another Seasonal Poem

You wail the word *winter*
as if it's the plague
that befalls year after year.
As if held witness
to the exodus of geese
heading southbound
and leaves floating serenely
to their end
rattles you to your core.
Sure the city suffers
seasonal dementia,
its colours bleached
by a collusion of clouds
in a climatic prank,
eased at a more
vulnerable hour
by manufactured
consumerism
and mass ritualization
of myth.

So what? Relax. Exhale.
Watch water vapour
rise from your mouth
like a miniature smokestack.
Walk in any direction
to make granola sounds
in the snow.

Look at the brotherhood of birch
in the backyard,
bare and battle-scarred.
Stiff as corpses.

For a moment
Death wants the limelight.
Before we can breathe again.
Before we can start over.

We Are Bioluminescent

My body contains enough fat
to make at least seven bars of soap.
The average person lives for
more than two billion seconds.
More synapses connect our galaxy
of neuronal constellations
than there are stars in the Milky Way.
Some of my atoms may have
occupied space on another planet.
These facts don't add value to my life.
Dust molecules gather while I
reproduce photocopies before lunch.
Manmade light moving faster
than my eyes. Analyzing
my environment through the lens
of science doesn't attract
me the way I had hoped.
Neither does the oceanside view
splashed on the magazine cover,
nor the surf of anticipation the moment
I encounter another wave of love.
Still, I wake to walk through it all
so desire can ignite my blood
as time humbles my bones.

Passage

O my mortal horse
proud and grey-eyed,
deaf and shag-eared.
How many troughs
and streams
have you drunk from,
returned to
never the same?
You low-hanging fruit,
cursed with a quad
of cracked
cloven hooves,
gorge for a back.
Gone is the engine,
the power
we compare to you.
The feed
that fuelled
your fondness.
Appetite,
but no will left
to dominate
the feral herd,
to take you storming
across the gilded
fields of desire.

II

Struggling Protagonist

In the beginning God created sound
and used it as a blunt object.
He gave some animals wings
but no hope of flying.
Others he banished to the ocean
too hideous for his eyes.
He made science a red herring
for skeptics and philosophers
so he could take the form of gadfly
sloshing through wine, buzzing into Athenian
bathhouses and Roman forums.
None of these things made him happy.
Now God takes the form
of a wild horse galloping over hills
or a flower in a field waiting to be plucked.
Sometimes he's the wind whistling above water
wishing his reflection would appear.

Indelible

The Internet informs me at 5,300 years Ötzi
the Iceman is the oldest body with tattoos.

Smoking outside Our Lady of Mercy, a man's scribed
a Jesus fish onto the canvas of his sunburnt arm.

Inside the gym, a boy with an explosion of veins
pulls his dumbbell closer to his heart, flexes *Ezekiel 25:17.*

A woman with a bumper sticker, *What would Jesus do?*
cuts me off in traffic, and I wonder how would Jesus

feel about his name being incorporated, bled over
billboards, *I'll Be Back* printed on t-shirts,

his followers immortalizing themselves in scripture
to ensure they too are not forgotten.

Sizing Up

I was given a reed like a measuring rod and was told,
"Go and measure the temple of God and the altar,
with its worshippers."
—REVELATION 11:1

If temptation of fruit in the garden
was knowledge, then John's reed

was power. He wielded it like a mad
sorcerer of shame: castigating

worshippers of the chosen—
prophets, farmers, peasants—

into belittlement. Such overbearing
administration of judgement.

When word reached God, He chuckled,
told John to put away his rod.

John complied begrudgingly.
Measured himself. Found himself lacking.

The Light Salesmen

They came on a Saturday
wearing their Sunday best.
They came ringing bells
with songs in their lungs.
They came high on resolve,
itching for ears. They came
before my first coffee. They
came when I was not dressed,
eating peanut butter on toast.
When my mind was miserable
and misunderstood, they came.
They came when I was afraid
of honesty and the best of me
was hiding. They came
waltzing in with wings, with
fireflies in the belly, hawking
broken flashlights. They spoke
of the Electrician. Asked if
I'd seen him, wondered if
I was looking, and how long I'd
been in the dark. They claimed
to know his whereabouts.
Offered me a map with his
coordinates. I remained silent,
holding the door. *How could
I say no to salvation?*

Prayer in the Age of Unreason

Let go of the willing captives. The reborn followers.
Even the cruelest deserve to know you don't exist.
Bring forth the freedom made by your absence.
Make a promise and keep it. Take this cup of
truth and drink from it. Swish this salt of surrender
inside your mouth. Multiply skeptics far and wide.
Flood newfound wisdom across these deserts
of prayer. O Lord, like a good hero, ride your horse
into that sunset and never turn back.

Mary Too

Did Mary give
consent to Gabriel

or did God just
decide for her?

When she conceived
did she feel violated?

When her body
pushed

did she think
why me?

A priest presses
the moon onto my tongue

like a stone
for the stomach.

I get no answers.

Kneeling on the plank
at my pew

I look up to see
a granite man

stuck to a cross,

hung
chain-linked

from the ceiling.

Outside
alone in the courtyard

his marble mother
weeping.

Sacrificial Sons

Heavy the feet in fear
the shaky
hands of Abraham

Doubt in the balance
of his head
Isaac in his grip

a stubborn desert
and the long walk
up Mount Moriah

Tension absolved
when God revealed
a bad joke

Years later
God to his own son
on the same mount
whispered

Let them nail you
            to wood

How many fathers since
have run a blade
through kin?

Another reason
for testimony:
need only point
      skyward shouting

He told me to!

Eternal Optimist

One must imagine Sisyphus happy.
—ALBERT CAMUS

take away the boulder
leave his two good feet

even if only the mountain
he is tasked with both directions

the trick is to believe
he heads solely skyward,

climbing that unreachable peak,
unable to turn or cling to thought,

unable to sift salt from scripture,
context from circumstance,

unable to decipher the sleepy world
from the book governed by

impractical gods
who burn forests for leisure,

rattle earth like a snow globe
in their leviathan fingers

the trick is to believe Atlas holds
more than earth together

that life is not a treadmill

the trick is not to look the future
in the eye

and count the bodies falling
from the sky, shadows flailing

over bridges or into trains

the trick is to deny the weight
of your shoulders

the wildfire in your head

and the ground below so hungry
and you never stopping

to look behind

to see the distance
between rock bottom

and what keeps you
bounding onward

Land in the Name of Taking

we harden in the arms
of faith. barbed wire fingers.
stone faces. rebar ribcages.
everything I know about honour
is buried in the ground. even
tonight while I make dreams
missiles are making music in
the skies over Gaza. forged
absolution from an air strike.
silence stacks silence on the
rubble and remains. blood
creeps through the streets.
men burn calories for war.
God's figurines lay expendable
in his sandbox. not one chosen
among others, lifted by his hands
pulled beyond the clouds.

Suffering as Spectacle

horsemen rode into ground   disappeared into clouds of blood

and hooves   the sun shrieked   a siren of earth broke into tremor

and tore sinew from muscle   beasts of a thousandfold erupted

enveloped light   we knelt for light   we braced for scorn and scourge

affliction debasement abandonment   appointed sacrifices

amidst our bygone memories of song   we scraped the sky

with our hands   scoured the surviving fruit   pleaded the beasts

to have mercy   as if they hungered for clemency   the beasts

only licked themselves   summoned a brief suspension

from their pilgrimage of puritanical hellfire   alone in attendance

God showered in wine   the tears and screams distilled for him

Holes

We fill in the holes with a bird's wing or a soldier's lung,

stand mouth agape looking at the gap in the sky.

What hell we found here hauled in overnight

to take away our dreams, the hole we dropped

ourselves into. This whole body does not remain.

What holy rots in us now? What war weaves into us

worse than reason? What militaristic monster rises?

Whose faith of a foreign kind? What father peddles

his son out for parlour tricks? What war incites children

to sea believing the waters will part? What's holier

than a man bearing a crown of explosives, mind

full of virgins, driving his holy through the heart

of the next home? What's holier than a vale of limbs

on the side of a holy war? What's holy now?

Hard Rain

With his tractor tires trenched in the mud
The farmer wept as his cows were swept by the flood

When clouds lashed out from above, the president
played golf while his people lost their city to the flood

A boy sulked over sunken ships in his tub
When God cried they had to name it the Great Flood

My father hid his depression out of love
Our basement revealed its secrets in the flood

I won't build an ark of fear if water comes
Earth's a droplet, not a tear, when it floods

Sonnet in Defence of Lust

We read our bodies in the basement.
Our fingers scribed notes in our skin.
We filled margins of the Bible
with urgency. They named us sinners.
Perdition is common perjury.
Why worship at the same altar
as hate? The test of a man's testament
is permission. So what if I've coveted
the flesh of a thousand strangers.
Binged on beauty at the feast of youth.
Love is saccharine not sacred. How
many loves have been lost not loving?
When I breathe in my last breath,
I won't be reminded of faith by death.

Nothing Written Is Sacred

They walk in crystalline civility
with comforting constraints.
They walk into buses and buildings
wearing ball bearings, pushing
buttons. With dislocated doctrines
they stumble through doors,
carrying acrobatic Bibles,
spitting God's spell. O tangle
of awkward tongues.
O slur of slipped speech.
Unspool these yarns of yammer,
this throng of tendrils.
Wake up, zealous city!
Turn off your repressive
apparatuses. Rise with your
gilded books of Science.
Your secular sheaths.
Rise in your machinery
of mischief, materializing
nuclear logic. O sensible
fundamentalist. O pious heretic.
Let reason rise through the wreckage.

III

Gun Journal

I

In church
during prayer,

maybe
our Lord's,

I pressed
my palms

wove
my fingers

pointed
my indexes

Bang bang, Mommy!
Bang bang!

II

neighbourhood
magic trick:

one man
made another's
life disappear

name found
in the local
newspaper

III

my parents
never
spoke of
them

them
being
one of those things
you
never
spoke of

IV

hiding under
the long hair
of a willow tree
by the lake
last to be found

You're dead!
I felt gun's
language,
its breath
a tiny cloud

v

I heard a gun shout
several houses down

followed by
           stumbling
silhouettes

           feet
forgetting themselves

VI

news story:
six-year-old

found a gun
between sofa cushions,

held its cold skin
in her hands,

mouthed its name
like gospel

before making
it sing

VII

last time
I heard one

spent an hour
on the bedroom floor
          in army crawl

                    waiting,
wading
through thoughts,

prayers

Safety Rules

after Kyle Dargan

Treat every man as if he could be loaded. Always keep a man
unloaded until you are ready to use him. Never point a man
at anything unless you intend to destroy it. There are no
second chances with a man. The purpose is to create safe
man-handling habits, and to discourage presumptive reasoning
along the lines of, "I know my man is unloaded so certain
unsafe practices are okay." In indoor areas where men will be
handled often, a suitably safe direction should be designated.
Wear, faulty assembly, damage or faulty design of the man
can cause him not to function as intended. Men may undergo
catastrophic failure (a "kaBoom") due to various causes. Many
families keep a man in the home. Young children are curious.
Even if you have talked to them many times about man safety,
they can't truly understand how dangerous men are. If they
come across a loaded man, they can accidentally hurt or kill
themselves or someone else. Teens can be emotional and may
act without thinking. If they have depression or are feeling
down, they may see a man as an easy way out. Men are dangerous.
They can hurt or even kill someone you know. Make sure
those around you follow the safety rules.

The Strongman

February 1939, New York, New York

Born, but barely, with bad breathing
The Mighty Atom bent horseshoes,

Pounded nails with his bare hands,
Busted chains by expanding his chest,

Even forced a fired bullet to flatten
Against his forehead. Swarmed by eighteen

Anti-Semites in Manhattan, he swatted
Them away with a Hebrew Hammer

Signature baseball bat. Later declared,
It wasn't a fight. It was a pleasure.

The Activist

June 1963, Cambridge, Maryland

Her hand pushed aside his muzzle
The way pretty girls do petty advances

More than carnations placed in barrels
Or fervent demonstrations of defiance

Despite *half fear, half God*
Her countenance wore confidence

For what is protest without
A gesture toward equality

To share, even for a moment,
What it means to be made invisible

Eyes of the Assailant

He does not name it *Monster*
but knows it is. Claws raised,
teeth serrated, salivating
in a corner down a corridor
in his skull. Even if he hides it,
locked up in his room of shame,
he feeds it. Makes its angry mouth
a tuba. Sometimes it climbs out
of him to bite the world on the ankle.
He wonders if it isn't so bad to be
beastly. What is desire without a
song of flesh? An engine of feeling?
Why the chase? Why antlers
if not to nail above a mantelpiece?
Why not a boy to inherit this hunger,
to take what he wants in his jaws?

Good Men

In my dream, the Devil tells me,
"There are no heroes in heaven."
A lie I believe to be true. Always
another mask behind a man.
Someone whom we've forgotten
to be anxious about. Good men
aren't avengers or caped crusaders,
vigilantes on a quest for justice.
They don't place pride ahead
of responsibility. Good men
stay home at night collecting
the words whispered by their lover.
Hold them until all fears disappear,
all faith in fidelity restored.
Good men turn the locks of their fists,
palms of vulnerability shining.

Colonial Chokehold

Milk is white.
A pillow is white.
A lamb. A church. A lie.
The White House.
The racism racing its heartbeat.
A hood used as a mask. The white cross
is red with blood.

A cloud is white.
A dove. A field of cotton.
An angel. An angel of death
is white. Columbus. Small pox.
A Black Robe was white.
Jesus was not
white.

Supremacy is white.
Privilege and patriarchy.
The Third Reich was white.
Donald Trump. Donald Trump
is white.

This poem. Even this.

Fallen

Build and it shall be built.
Drink and you shall get drunk

in a witnessing tent,
      wine-washed away to sleep,
your 500-year-old body,
naked, vomit-stained.

Could you smell the water
in your dreams,   was it guilt
that led you here?

The stench of God's filthy animals,
the sins that walked away with you
from the ark?

Were there ghosts in ghastly visions,
a silt bed of bony corpses
      obstructing thoughts of sea?

What awoke in you
     to plant grape seed,
to sacrifice reputation like a lamb?

Speak frail hero,   speak Noah.

Have you heard
what your sons call you?

Superhero AA

He arrives late wearing his civilian costume,
sits in the last chair in our circle. George is rambling,
kicking around a tired story like a Hacky Sack—
something about his ex-wife, a final notice
and too many Coors Lights. When the floor is his
he cracks his concrete knuckles, stares
at his steel-toed boots, introduces himself
and recites the code, "Hulk here. Alcoholic."
Begins chartering his past: each morning
waking up shirtless, head an explosion of anvils,
waist-deep in destruction. Today though, progress.
When he felt rage (roommate insulting his lady—
comment about thunder thighs) instead
of running his roommate's face through drywall
he ran a bath. "You know I never considered
myself a bubble bath guy." We cork our laughter
before it spills, generously applaud his efforts
toward anger management, plunge our stories
into nostalgia: plastic ships, rubber ducks,
so as not to put ourselves in any hot water.

Epistle of the Inebriate

I went to the worst of bars

              to drink with the other animals,

    lifted the glass to my mouth

and I drank deeply, I drank so deeply.

             My head neolithic,

river of speechless current,

listening to the in-between despite the abyss at the edge of the table.

       As the empty cans dropped out of our paws

something caught inside our throats was released—some old grief,

       sprung from the head of a thousand-fisted wretch.

Vomiting it all up on Pearse Street,

    tossing off expletives into the sea of cab lights,

      leaning on one another, too tired to go home.

Empty

For drink, sirs, is not disease
but desire. Such crippling company.
One cannot retire on desire
with disease. I do not Bible
but I bleed. What breath
                              is left for brains
and who asked for bread? For Bibles
          sealed in babble, sworn in bed.
Please, more. Poor me, help.
Help pour another please. Please
another pour. What faith I have
slurred. What faith I have left to face.
What is faith to me? What's left of
my face?

Ode to Ruin

My habit put a bottle to my head
and told me to drink. So I drank
to serve the habit. My habit keeps
me honest, keeps me sane. My habit
put a hit on my sorrow. Sorrow who
sinks me, sorrow who swells in me
a bloated gospel of confusion.
My habit lifts my glass, lifts me up.
A toast to my habit! I am one
with my habit. O habit! My habit!
My darling habit. Habit of my heart.

Drowning Man Sonnets

I drink to drown my sorrows,
but the accursed things have learned how to swim.
— JOSÉ FRÍAS

I

Earliest memories: bewitched
by ant colonies, the inverted
world from monkey bars,
spell of the ice-cream truck jingle.
Introduced to urgency by the *Playboy*
found near an oak tree. First sign
of desperation when bitten by a nail,
its rusty tooth puncturing his sneaker.
At twelve, lost and alone, he flooded
a French train station with his tears.
At fourteen, met his future nemesis.
Wrapped his hands around
its throat, twisted then drank
as addiction took root in his blood.

II

Booze was a rite of passage to
impress the guys, to gather the
guts to ask out the girl. He chased
spirits until it tired his blood,
bashing him like a fourth-liner's fist.
When he got older it became his
sole companion—a buddy to
band-aid struggle, brighten life's
shitty weather. *Pour whisky on the
wound*, they told him. So he did.
With his room as his witness
he drank four-hundred days
and four-hundred nights,
floating in the lifeboat of the lost.

III

After raking the scattered freckles
on his arm, he begins prying his nails
like incised cans, rolling back
shores of hygiene, tearing cuticles
in the process, leaving clefts for
the armies of bacteria. It's his
anxiety's duty—peeling skin
with a paring knife. Pain entering
nerve, fluid escaping, body relaxing.
Defying reality fiction succumbs to.
Bleeding is his silent resistance.
Healing a continual compromise.
Breaking flesh a metaphor
for this uncomfortable acceptance.

IV

Trapped in the well of his body
paralysis prompted by inflictions
of memory and rivers and fields
glassed over with ice and frost
he wrangles the rope of thought,
and pulls—*pills* they say, *my pills,*
my pills he repeats his lungs emerge
as if rising from a lake or swamp
what fear the head fought
what battle lingered in the teeth
wounded from gnash and gnaw
with suspicions nagging, pulling
in a voice that's his but not his
but like a child's or a god's.

V

He drops a match on his wound to set fire
to his blood. At a certain temperature even
the Devil cools. Any horror can drown in the fens
of a depressant. A ghost hums its dark dictionary,
its sharp symphony of terrible. Monsters wake
to feast on the horses in his heart. His body
an inane language—glossolalia, gibberish.
He tramples hardwood. Bruises wall paint.
Thoughts clamber the stone well of synapses
chasing fumes from chemical birds. His mind
unmoored, feet divine, dancing on a dead sea
in a porcelain tub. Surrounded by sludge in
a chamber of billowing murk, he lights another
flame to channel the voices chanting his name.

VI

Like Mad Max he tears across
suburban roadway, accosting
medians and commercial lots.
Tires breach every line. To the liquor
store as the crow flies. Employees
brace for impact but he brakes
in time to jump out, race through
the doors, straight to his addiction.
Hastens toward the cashier.
Mutters *Thanks*. Leaves drunk.
Returns drunk. Fills up every hour.
Each time more staggered, less
coherent. Mumbling, wobbling until
the floor sucker punches him to sleep.

Drowning Man is not a superhero. He's the amazing
alcoholic with no power of responsibility.
Wears an idle cape of despair. Armed with denial
and self-destruction. Drinks to forget his shame
of drinking. Cradles his kryptonite to sleep.
Walks through time machines to speak primitive
tongue with strangers. To engage in knuckle psalm.
Fist verse. He once awoke in a field and thought
he landed on the moon. Looked up to see the astronaut's
lightbulbs and a bright stream of fuselage tailing
a lone vessel. His therapist called this a shooting star.
Said he was inspired by the superpower of motion
blindness. But Drowning Man knows what he saw:
a hero hurtling through space, gifted to a sober planet.

VIII

He wades in the polluted basin of his own
making, summoning words from black matter.
His apartment is a scrapyard of tangents.
Some nights he's a sacrifice for the savages
in his head. On well-medicated ones an iridescence
of snowflakes. A field of luminous lanterns. Opens
the night sky with electric intentions. Swigs from
seductive liquors, pulling vermillion scarves
from his mouth. A city explodes into possibilities.
A glance becomes an invitation, becomes a touch,
becomes a dreamscape. His body enters another
and yearns to release. A rapturous blur. Moments
unburdened by the cloak of self-consciousness.
A portal of escape from his own misadventures.

IX

She lines up a village of glass stowaways
one by one on the slick marble countertop.
Watches the guilt run its course through
his veins. He feels the horror creep along
the backs of his eyelids. The sacrament of
its foul kiss, its serpentine tongue, expelled.
This, his liquid kingdom. Pillaged. Purified.
This dark cathedral shaken. Its barbaric Bible
burned. She unveils the vice that operates his
slaving machinations. His mouth surrenders
to silence as if held at gunpoint. A swell of
shame rises. His face inflames. He hurls
a chair into the cheekbone of the floor.
Let them out, she whispers. *Watch the devils run.*

X

Instead of sipping the blood of Jesus on Sunday
he flocks the church of alcohol. Holy grail =
Old Milwaukee = Drowning Man has a problem.
Step one: therapy. *Stop drinking. See you in two weeks.*
How did it go? Stop drinking. See you in two weeks. How
did it go? Stop drinking. See you in two weeks. How did
it go? Stop drinking. See you in two weeks. How did...
the mind become a wheel of unreason,
a loathsome ministry of self-medication.
Drowning Man is a wounded sparrow seeing
a wolf therapist. Step two: Alcoholics Anonymous.
Surrender to the will of God. Step three: peddling
the broken bicycle of recovery Drowning Man
pours himself a drink. Considers his next option.

XI

Hovers over himself like a stubborn
rain cloud. Studies the sorcery of
rigor mortis. Skin—barren fields
of decomposition. A corpse appears
beyond recognition, as if inhabited
by a stranger. Recounts grandma's
funeral, her countenance a flower
without pigmentation. Weeks before
a stroke made half her face fall,
every tendon that kept muscle and
bone sinewed, let go in quiet relief.
He returns to his own physical history.
If the flesh is the last window into life,
his is an exhibition of self-loathing.

XII

At his worst when the bully in his brain
bruises him blue, blow after blow,
he fantasizes about bridges for diving.
Floods the river with toxins
so a Mariachi band can sing him
through to the end. He fears police
will raid his room, order him to drop
the dream. He rises to a floating
bed-frame, a desperate clock
trapped in his ear, wall-photo
manifestations of guilt. Clambers
to the balcony. Yells at the cacophony
of cars below. Jump is to make it stop.
To make everything recede from view.

XIII

What's hidden? Maybe more bottles
under the sink. Maybe the chewing tobacco
in the top kitchen cabinet. Maybe the lies
tucked under his tongue. Maybe truth
banging on the door, his mouth locked
by pride, too chicken shit to open.
Maybe a ship of sadness. The fear
of the monster asleep. Maybe an army
of locusts in his skin the strength
of a thousand itches. Maybe a violence
of thought restless in the attic. A collection
of madness in the dark. Maybe the heart
unable to repair. Maybe a body.
Maybe his own. Maybe. Maybe not.

XIV

On a seaside recovery tour he passes a pair
of vacant shoes worried about their missing feet.
Considers himself missing, unburdened with feeling.
His current machinery misfiring. Conscious of
serotonin's unreliable narrator. This vessel
he wants to burn and climb out from. Mind
laments the absence of drink. The echo of Narcissus
drowning in each bottle. Remembers his father,
the sun and the holy ghosts of neural networks.
He summons the god of strength and sobriety.
A seagull appears strolling aimlessly along the wharf.
Be T.S. Eliot. Be crablike. Abandon this shanty of unrest.
Without fault gashes. Without wrist rivers. These days
when the light is scarce, go inhabit another ark.

Notes

The opening epigraph is taken from *Daybreak: Thoughts on the Prejudices of Morality* by Friedrich Nietzsche (Cambridge University Press, 1997, p. 52).

"Sizing Up": Epigraph is taken from the New International Version of *The Bible* (Biblica, 2011).

"Eternal Optimist": Epigraph is taken from *The Myth of Sisyphus and Other Essays* by Albert Camus (Vintage Books, 1983, p. 123).

"Hard Rain": Shares the same title as a Tony Hoagland poem found in the collection *What Narcissism Means to Me* (Graywolf Press, 2003), that was originally inspired by the Bob Dylan song, "A Hard Rain's a-Gonna Fall" from the album *The Freewheelin' Bob Dylan* (Sony Records, 1963).

"Safety Rules": Found poem incorporating text from several gun owner manuals, journals and websites. It owes a lot to Kyle Dargan's "Minefields" published on *BuzzFeedNews.com* on September 20, 2016.

"The Strongman": Tribute to Joseph L. Greenstein, better known as the Mighty Atom. The Hebrew Hammer was a nickname for baseball star Hank Greenberg. The line in italics is a quote from Greenstein's statement after an altercation with eighteen members of the Nazi Bund on February 20, 1939 in midtown Manhattan (*The Mighty Atom: The Life and Times of Joseph L. Greenstein* by Ed Spielman, Viking Press, 1979).

"The Activist": Tribute to civil rights activist Gloria Richardson who was famously photographed walking past an armed US National Guardsman during a protest. The line in italics is a quote from Richardson in an interview she did with *The New York Times* ("50 Years After Dr. King's Death, Remembering the Women Who Steered the Movement" by Nikita Stewart, *NYTimes.com*, April 2, 2018).

"Epistle of the Inebriate": Cento that borrows lines from the following poets (in order of appearance): "the suicide kid" by Charles Bukowski, "Thirst" by Laura Cronk, "A Drinking Song" by W.B. Yeats, "Russian Ending" by Jerry Williams, "On Alcohol" by sam sax, "Square Cells" by Jenny Xie, "At the Blue Note" by Pablo Medina, "Jet" by Tony Hoagland, "The Best Drink" by Lee Upton, "A Bell, Still Unrung" by Safiya Sinclair, "A Copper Basin in Florence" by Lani O'Hanlon, "The News" by Wendy Xu, and "Scrambled Eggs" by Hayden Carruth.

"Drowning Man Sonnets": Epigraph is taken from *The Fabulous Life of Diego Rivera* by Bertram D. Wolfe (Cooper Square Press, 2000, p. 100).

Acknowledgments

MANY THANKS to the following journals, in which versions of these poems were first published:

"Struggling Protagonist" appeared in EVENT, Volume 50, Issue 1, April 2021 (forthcoming).

"Meditation on Enclosed Space" appeared in *Vallum*, Volume 17, Issue 1, "Home," April 2020.

"Driving Through Kitsilano" appeared online in *Savant-Garde*, Issue 2: Winter, January 2020.

"Epistle of the Inebriate" appeared online in *Unlost Journal*, Issue 19 "Signals," November 2019.

"Superhero AA" appeared online in *Unbroken Journal*, Issue 23, October 2019.

"Another Seasonal Poem" appeared online in *Juniper* in Volume 3, Issue 2, Fall, October 2019.

"Suburban Lament" appeared online in *talking about strawberries all of the time* in October 2019.

"Disciple" and "This Might Be the Warmest Parking Lot in Canada" appeared online in *Cascadia Rising Review* in Issue 5, Spring, April 2019.

"Prayer in the Age of Unreason" appeared online in *The Bookends Review* in March 2019.

"The Light Salesmen" appeared online in *Train* in December 2018.

"Drowning Man Sonnets" (IV) appeared as "House of Shadows" in *Train*, Print Issue 2, September 2018.

"Drowning Man Sonnets" (v, vi, viii, x, xi, xiii)
    appeared online, under different titles, in *Montréal
    Writes*, Volume 1, Issue 11, November 2018.
"Land in the Name of Taking" and "Suffering as
    Spectacle," under the title "Sadism as Prayer,"
    appeared online in *Mantra Review*, Volume 1, Issue 3,
    October 2018.
"Eternal Optimist" appeared in PRISM *international*,
    Volume 56, Issue 4, Summer 2018.
"Drowning Man Sonnets" (vii) appeared online as
    "Drowning Man is Not a Superhero" in *The Maynard*,
    Spring, Volume 11, Issue 1, February 2018.
"Two Lips" appeared online in *Sewer Lid*, Issue 2,
    October 2016.

Earlier versions of "Churches, Trucks and Shallow Pools"
(previously titled "Unbuckling the Bible Belt"), "Ode to the
Hockey Bro" and "Two Lips" appeared in the self-published
chapbook *Silo Society* (2016).

To the members of the Arts Council of New Westminster, the
City of New Westminster, Royal City Literary Arts Society,
Poetry in the Park and Poetry New Westminster, thank you all
for providing me with friendship and support.

To the staff and students at New Westminster Secondary
School, thank you for your energy and enthusiasm toward
education and learning.

To the CanLit poets whom I consider friends and
acquaintances, thank you for your time and company.

To my idols and mentors through verse, thank you for your language and inspiration.

To Alan Brownoff, Cathie Crooks, Michelle Lobkowicz, Duncan Turner and everyone at University of Alberta Press who helped make this book happen. I also want to thank my editor Kimmy Beach for her insightful feedback.

To family and friends in Abbotsford, Dublin, Perth, St. John's, Toronto and Vancouver, for being a part of my journey and endorsing my work.

To my loving parents, Alfred and Margaret.

To Marjali, forever, for always.

Other Titles from University of Alberta Press

The Bad Wife
MICHELINE MAYLOR
An intimate, first-hand account of how to ruin
a marriage.
Robert Kroetsch Series

Believing is not the same as Being Saved
LISA MARTIN
Lyric poems that tenderly meditate on life and
death, joy and sorrow, faith and doubt.
Robert Kroetsch Series

Too Bad
Sketches Toward a Self-Portrait
ROBERT KROETSCH
Governor General's Award-winning author shows
through stark lyric how "every enduring poem was
written today."
A volume in cuRRents, a Canadian literature series

More information at uap.ualberta.ca